**Gardeners'
World** magazine

101 Shade-loving Plants

10 9 8 7 6 5 4 3 2 1

Published in 2008 by BBC Books,
an imprint of Ebury Publishing
A Random House Group Company

The Random House Group Limited Reg. No. 954009

Addresses for companies within the Random House Group can be
found at www.randomhouse.co.uk

A CIP catalogue record for this book is available from the British Library.

The Random House Group Limited supports The Forest Stewardship
Council (FSC), the leading international forest certification organization.
All our titles that are printed on Greenpeace approved FSC certified
paper carry the FSC logo. Our paper procurement policy can be found
at www.rbooks.co.uk/environment

To buy books by your favourite authors and register for offers visit
www.rbooks.co.uk

Printed and bound by Firmengruppe APPL, aprinta druck,
Wemding, Germany
Colour origination by GRB Editrice Ltd., London

Commissioning Editor: Lorna Russell
Project Editor: Laura Higginson
Designer: Kathryn Gammon
Production: Bridget Fish
ISBN: 9781846074509

Gardeners' World magazine

101 Shade-loving Plants
IDEAS TO LIGHTEN SHADOWS

Author
James Wickham

Picture researcher
Janet Johnson

BOOKS

Contents

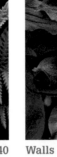

Introduction

Having shade in the garden is often seen as a tricky issue, but if you've got it, think yourself lucky. This is, in fact, a huge opportunity because many of our most exciting plants actually prefer to be in subdued light. In fact, every garden has areas of lower light levels from a shady wall or a spot overshadowed by trees or hedges to a fully north-facing garden in the lee of neighbouring buildings. But fear not, all these can be brightened with the right plants; read on and we'll show you how to do this.

In this book you'll find 101 favourite plants that will all thrive in shade. There's a chapter on ground-covering plants, another that highlights plants when they're overshadowed by walls, and one covering each season to prove that you really can have a shady garden that looks good all year round.

Among the plants that we at *Gardeners' World Magazine* have chosen for this book are fail-safe favourites, such as ferns and hostas, as well as many new and unusual plants to provide extra inspiration. You could call them all shady characters – but in the best possible way!

James Wickham
Gardeners' World Magazine

Shade plants tips

Choosing plants that are naturally shade-tolerant is the first step to success if you have a shady garden, but you can employ other tactics, which will really make a difference to the final result.

Shade is often caused by overhead trees or nearby hedges, which make the surrounding ground very impoverished, so it's essential to improve the soil before planting. The most effective soil improvers are garden compost or well-rotted farmyard manure, added generously to the soil when planting.

To help conserve moisture in a dry shady area, use a mulch of garden compost spread at least 5cm (2in) deep over the soil every year. You could also use a pale coloured gravel to do the same job and this has the added advantage of making a shady area seem instantly brighter.

Don't be afraid of raising up a tree's crown by taking off some lower branches and pruning off the bottom branches of established shrubs. This will let in loads more light, make the garden seem more spacious and often improve the shape of the plant as well.

Take advantage of the seasonality of shade cast by trees that lose their leaves in autumn. A huge range of winter and spring-flowering bulbs and perennials such as snowdrops, crocuses and hardy cyclamen will flower and grow happily while light can stream in through the bare canopy.

If choosing trees for a small garden plump for those with small leaves and light canopies, such as birches and rowans, as light will filter down through them allowing a greater range of plants to grow underneath. Upright or columnar-shaped trees such as the flagpole cherry, *Prunus* 'Amanogawa' also provide height without having a large spreading crown.

In a small shady town garden, paint walls or fences a pale colour to reflect any available light, or choose climbers with yellow or variegated leaves, such as *Hedera helix* 'Buttercup' to provide a bright background.

Hardy plants that have been grown in pots can be planted throughout the year, but they are much easier to establish if planted in the autumn or spring, while the ground is moist and warm. This is especially important if planting a dry shady garden.

A sprinkling of general-purpose fertiliser around the plants once a year will encourage quick establishment and healthy growth, especially in poorer soils.

Lawns can become very bare and mossy in a small shady garden, so it's often better to re-design the space, replacing the lawn with materials such as gravel or paving, softened with plants in beds and containers.

Anemone
Anemone blanda

A late-winter wake-up with bulbs

Time to plant: autumn
Bulb H: 10–20cm (4–8in), S: 15–30cm (6–12in)

This early spring-flowering anemone is easily grown and thrives in bare ground or sparse grass under trees, quickly naturalising into a wonderful patch of colour. Varieties with blue, pink and pristine white flowers are available and look gorgeous if planted together to form a little tapestry. Anemones also look lovely weaving among the sunny blooms of the winter aconite and the little propeller-shaped blooms of the hardy *Cyclamen coum*.

The hard, knobbly bulbs of *Anemone blanda*, correctly called tubers, should be planted shallowly in the soil in autumn, and be arranged in random groups for a natural effect.

TIP

If naturalising these bulbs in sparse grass, allow the anemone foliage to die back before mowing.

Camellia
Camellia x *williamsii* 'Contribution'

Classic camellia

Time to plant: all year round
Shrub H: 90cm (3ft), S: 90cm (3ft)

The aristocrats of the early spring garden, camellias bring style and glamour at a time of year when it's most unexpected and welcome. The waxy blooms almost look too tender to be outside, but this is a tough evergreen that shrugs off winter cold and thrives in quite deep shade.

All camellias prefer acid soil, but don't let that put you off if you have more limy conditions at home, as they grow perfectly well in containers filled with ericaceous compost. If you can, place your pot away from the morning sun as a rapid thaw after a frosty night can damage the flowers.

To keep leaves a lustrous dark green, remember to feed pot-grown camellias during summer with a fertiliser for ericaceous plants. Keep pot-grown camellias damp at all times in summer, as drying out even for a short time may cause them to drop their plump, unopened flower buds the following spring.

TIP
Camellias don't need regular pruning, but if your plant becomes too large it will respond well to pruning and will sprout again, even from an old stump.

Mexican orange blossom
Choisya 'Aztec Pearl'

Scent for spring gardens

Time to plant: all year round
Shrub H: 2.4m (8ft), S: 2.4m (8ft)

Worth growing just for its aromatic evergreen leaves, this lovely shrub also produces clusters of scented white flowers in late spring. In most years you'll also get another, smaller flush of blooms in autumn.

Mexican orange blossom is perfectly happy in part-shade, for example against an east-facing wall where it will get sun for the early part of the day. It can also make a beautiful specimen plant when grown in a large pot of soil-based compost. Well-drained soil is essential.

Although sometimes slow to get established, the Mexican orange blossom can eventually reach about head height and the same across, so allow plenty of room when planting. Like the better-known Mexican orange blossom (*Choisya ternata*) this variety can be kept more compact by pruning back the shoots after flowering in late spring.

TIP
Young plants can be easily raised from cuttings taken from new shoots in summer.

Corydalis
Corydalis flexuosa

Cool blues for shade

Time to plant: all year round
Perennial H: 30cm (12in), S: 20cm (8in)

Darts of electric-blue shimmer above the ferny foliage of this choice perennial for weeks in late spring and summer. This corydalis is a relatively new introduction from China, but it has rapidly become a favourite plant because of its exquisite colour and love of cool, shady places.

Corydalis is not that fussy about soil, and flourishes in loose, compost-enriched soil where it will spread into a gorgeous, lush pool of foliage and flowers. After a long season of flowers, the whole plant then takes a well-deserved rest and dies down, sprouting fresh leaves again in autumn.

You can obtain extra plants very easily by digging up and detaching pieces from an established clump in spring, and planting them straight away in another part of the garden. Alternatively pot them up for a while first.

TIP
Plant alongside *Brunnera macrophylla* 'Jack Frost' and epimediums to provide plenty of interest in summer when the corydalis takes a break.

Bleeding heart
Dicentra spectabilis

Delicate perennials for dappled light

Time to plant: all year round
Perennial H: 1.2m (4ft), S: 45cm (18in)

Elegance oozes from this easily grown perennial in late spring, when tiny heart-shaped flowers nod from the underside of arching stems. Its ferny leaves perfectly complement the flowers and emerge first with the stems as a translucent pink colour, maturing to a beautiful sea green.

Bleeding heart thrives in a cool, shady border, whether it gets shade for some of the day or dappled light throughout. Ensure the roots remain damp in summer by adding plenty of garden compost to the soil when planting, and also use it as a mulch around the plant every spring.

There is also a very pretty white-flowered variety of bleeding heart – *Dicentra spectabilis* 'Alba' – whose little flowers beam out from a shady border like rows of newly laundered pantaloons.

TIP
Bleeding heart has quite long, fleshy roots, and hates to be disturbed once established.

Shooting star
Dodecatheon clevelandii

Stars of spring

Time to plant: all year round
Perennial H: 40cm (16in), S: 15cm (6in)

Floral aerodynamics take place above the leaves of this perennial in spring, as its flowers open like a shower of brightly coloured shooting stars. The best display can be had from a plant that is grown in a little shade, where its roots remain cool and slightly damp in the summer months.

Despite its exotic appearance, the shooting star is closely related to the primrose and cowslip, and it is just as easy to grow. On drier soils it benefits from a deep mulch of garden compost every spring. This is also the time to divide plants, which is worth doing every few years in order to keep the clump vigorous and flowering well.

TIP
Take precautions against slugs and snails, which can damage the young leaves in spring.

Dog's tooth violet
Erythronium revolutum

A joyous splash of colour

Time to plant: autumn
Bulb H: 30cm (12in), S: 10cm (4in)

Swept-back pink petals, shaped like a miniature Turk's cap, give great character to this graceful erythronium. A natural woodland plant, it relishes the cool, dappled shade under trees or large shrubs and loves deep, compost-enriched soil.

Although the flowers only last a few, short weeks in spring, the leaves are also a joy. Often handsomely marbled with dark spots, they give the plant its common name of trout lily in its native America. In Britain it has the common name of dog's tooth violet, which refers to the fang-like shape of its bulbs.

Dog's tooth violet can be slow to establish, but once it does you'll find that it self-seeds and creates a spreading colony. Dry bulbs can be obtained in autumn, and these should be planted as soon as possible to prevent them drying out too much.

TIP
Label or make a note of the place where you plant bulbs as they die back quickly after flowering. This avoids accidentally digging them up.

Spurge
Euphorbia 'Blackbird'

Vibrant contrasting colours to perk up shady corners

Time to plant: all year round
Perennial H: 50cm (20in), S: 50cm (20in)

Extra-dark maroon leaves provide a striking background to the lime-green flowers of this lovely new euphorbia. These densely arranged leaves are also evergreen, so they make a great contribution to the winter garden. Like many euphorbias, 'Blackbird' thrives in shade, although the leaf colour will be darker if the plant gets sun for some of the day.

Vibrant red flower stems stretch above the foliage in late spring, clasping the contrasting green flowers. The colourful outer parts of the flower are actually bracts, which are leafy in texture and last for many weeks. These can eventually be snipped off when they fade in late summer, but wear gloves to do this as the cut stems ooze a milky sap that can be an irritant if it gets on the skin.

TIP
The compact habit of this new euphorbia makes it perfect for pots. It looks especially good in winter with bronze-leaved grasses and warm orange pansies.

Hacquetia
Hacquetia epipactis

An emerald glow in dark days

Time to plant: all year round
Perennial H: 5cm (2in), S: 15–30cm (6–12in)

Subtle and sophisticated, the green flowers of this choice perennial arrive, rather endearingly, on the cusp of spring. The bright emerald-green petals of hacquetia are in fact a ruff of leafy bracts, which means they last for ages. The real flowers are found in the neat golden button in the centre.

This pretty perennial thrives in a shady border and looks lovely in a woodland garden. As it is a petite plant, place it at the front of a bed or border so that you can fully appreciate its flowers and to prevent other plants smothering its compact charm.

Hacquetia is easily grown and needs very little regular attention, other than snipping off any dead leaves in winter. Additional plants are easy to obtain; simply lift and divide an established plant in spring.

TIP
Hacquetias like their roots to stay cool and damp in summer, so add plenty of compost to the soil when planting to help retain moisture.

Hepatica
Hepatica transsilvanica 'Eisvogel'

A woodland white for early spring

Time to plant: all year round
Perennial H: 15cm (6in), S: 20cm (8in)

Sparkling white flowers make this little woodland plant a jewel in the early spring garden. White flowers are a little unusual for a hepatica as the blooms of most types are in shades of blue or pink. White is, however, one of the colours that shows up best in a shady area.

All the hepatica family are happiest in dappled shade, and although some are quite petite, this variety is a robust perennial that's ideal for the front of a cool border, even under trees. It loves compost-enriched soil, so add plenty when planting and it will soon form a gorgeous spread of white flowers.

The lobed leaves of this hepatica eventually make a handsome clump. Once established, this plant will flower best if left undisturbed, and it needs very little regular care at all, apart from snipping off dead leaves in winter.

TIP
Hepatica looks stunning with the contrasting foliage of *Hakonechloa macra* 'Aureola', a Japanese grass with swishy golden blades that also does well in shade.

Forget-me-not
Myosotis

A free-flowering bed of blue

Time to plant: summer
Perennials but treat as biennials; various heights

An exuberance of sky-blue flowers on this pretty bedding plant create a frothy effect that is just perfect for use as an under-storey to the tall, satiny chalices of tulips. Forget-me-nots are also extremely useful in covering bare soil between emerging perennials, and will self-sow into areas of dappled shade under trees.

The taller blue varieties, such as 'Royal Blue', are far more natural-looking than the extremely dwarf types, which are really only suitable for pots. All are very easy to grow from seed: sow them in pots outdoors in early summer, transplant into individual pots and then plant out into the garden later in summer. They will then flower the following spring. Once flowering is over, pull the whole plant up as forget-me-nots are best treated as biennials and replaced every year. (You will find that they usually self-seed so you don't have to raise new plants.)

TIP
Forget-me-nots are a good choice for a shady, wildlife-friendly garden among plants such as comfrey and honesty.

Lesser celandine
Ranunculus ficaria 'Brazen Hussy'

A dark treat for dull corners

Time to plant: spring
Perennial H: 5cm (2in), S: 30cm (12in)

Discovered by chance in the wild by the late plantsman Christopher Lloyd, this variety of lesser celandine has wickedly dark, chocolatey leaves that set off its glinting golden flowers a treat. Unlike the ordinary lesser celandine, which can be a bit of a spreading nuisance, 'Brazen Hussy' is much better behaved. It likes the same shady places as its weedier relative.

'Brazen Hussy' is just one of a few named varieties of the lesser celandine, including the delightful 'Collarette' with petite, double orange flowers and 'Brambling', which has silver and chocolate patterned leaves. They are all lovely to use in alpine sinks among small winter and early spring bulbs, such as *Crocus tommasinianus*, *Cyclamen coum* and *Iris reticulata*. Growing them in a container has the added advantage of giving you time to assess how quickly the plants are increasing, before you plant them out in the garden.

TIP
All varieties of lesser celandine naturally die back in summer, so if you are growing them in the garden, mark the spot carefully to avoid accidentally digging them up when dormant.

Bloodroot
Sanguinaria canadensis f. *multiplex* 'Plena'

Pristine rosettes double the impact

Time to plant: spring
Perennial H: 15cm (6in), S: 30cm (12in)

Double flowers are rarely more alluring than on this little woodland plant. Each bloom is a perfect rosette of pristine white petals, opening rather unusually only a few centimetres from the ground. The beautifully scalloped, greyish-green leaves unfurl fully just after the flowers but they don't last long and naturally die back for the summer.

In its native America, *Sanguinaria canadensis* is known as bloodroot, because the underground rhizomes ooze red sap when cut. The ordinary single-flowered species. *S. canadensis*, is also very charming but its flowers last even less time than the double variety.

Any moist, compost-enriched soil in a cool, shady position suits this choice perennial, and in these conditions it will thrive. Once your plant is established you can think about dividing it to produce more plants. This should be done in autumn so that you don't damage the buds nosing through the soil in spring.

TIP
Take precautions against slugs, which can damage the young, emerging flower buds in spring.

Wake robin
Trillium sessile

Woodland gem

Time to plant: all year round for pot-grown plants
Perennial H: 30cm (12in), S: 20cm (8in)

Style comes naturally to this lovely perennial, thanks to its gorgeous trio of mottled leaves over which the dark flowers are snugly centred, like a precious jewel laid out for display. Best of all, wake robin revels in a shady border, especially in loose, leafy soil that doesn't dry out too much in summer.

Like all members of this highly esteemed family, *Trillium sessile* can be slow to grow into a decent-sized clump, but even a small plant will provide immense pleasure when its wonderful foliage and flowers unfurl in late spring.

The trillium's slow growth makes it a little hard to come by sometimes, but it is well worth searching out. Look out for the white flowered *T. grandiflorum*, which can be a bit easier to find and looks fantastic if planted in the bare ground under trees.

TIP
Leave trilliums undisturbed once established, digging up a piece only for your most cherished friend!

Large merrybells
Uvularia grandiflora

A mouthwatering treat with zesty flowers and lush foliage

Time to plant: all year round
Perennial H: 75cm (30in), S: 30cm (12in)

Closely related to Solomon's seal, this American woodland plant shares a similar, quiet elegance, as its dainty lemon bells nod shyly from the tops of its stems in late spring. The twisted lemon petals don't last that long, but the whole plant is immensely graceful in a shady border.

Cool, damp soil is bliss to *Uvularia grandiflora*, in which it will soon increase into a lush and beautiful specimen. Once established it doesn't need much regular attention, other than cutting down the old stems in late autumn. Keep a close watch out for slugs in spring as they find the new shoots particularly tasty.

You can get a few extra plants for free by digging up and dividing a plant in early spring, just before the new shoots start emerging.

TIP
As its flowering season is short, plant something close by for later interest. Bulbs, such as colchicums, are ideal as their huge, crocus-like flowers emerge in autumn.

Columbine
Aquilegia vulgaris var. *stellata* 'Nora Barlow'

Add a touch of old-fashioned charm

Time to plant: all year round
Perennial H: 90cm (3ft), S: 45cm (18in)

Beloved in cottage gardens, in summer the aquilegia exudes charm from dainty, nodding blooms stretching above gorgeous, ferny foliage. 'Nora Barlow' is one of the most popular varieties of aquilegia, with exquisitely pleated double flowers that perfectly suit its other common name – granny's bonnet.

All aquilegias flourish in dappled shade and are very much at home in a woodland garden, where they will usually naturalise by self-seeding, once established. This is a bonus because individual plants can be short-lived, however, the seedlings will usually vary in colour because aquilegias are highly promiscuous and readily hybridise with other types. Whatever the colour, though, all have a natural grace and you may even find one that is better than the original.

TIP
To prevent an excess of seedlings, especially in small gardens, deadhead most of the flowers, leaving just a few to set seed.

Astilbe
Astilbe 'Irrlicht'

Light up shady corners with pale plumes

Time to plant: all year round
Perennial H: 50cm (20in), S: 50cm (20in)

In summer, wiry stems (which never need support) hold aloft the plume-like flowerheads of this easily grown perennial. Provided the soil remains moist, astilbes are happy in partial shade, and although there are many pink and red varieties, this white one really shines out from a gloomy border.

Astilbes are all long-lived, reliable plants that get bigger and better every year. Occasionally mature clumps will benefit from being divided, and this is best done in early spring, just as new growth begins. Once you have dug up the plant, cut through the crown with a sharp knife or spade, as it can be quite woody. Replant strong pieces back into compost-enriched soil and water them in well.

The fern-like foliage of astilbes is extremely beautiful and often emerges a rich bronze-red. These leaves can also add autumn colour. Plants with contrasting leaves, such as round, leathery bergenias and the slender sheaves of *Iris sibirica*, make complimentary neighbours.

TIP
Wait until spring before cutting down this plant, as the old plumes turn warm chestnut-brown in winter and look fantastic in frosty weather.

Masterwort

Astrantia major 'Roma'

Cover shady ground with a splash of lively pink

Time to plant: all year round
Perennial H: 1m (3¼ft), S: 60cm (2ft)

A ruff of clear pink bracts cradling a pincushion of tiny, quivering pink flowers gives this hearty perennial plenty of charisma in the summer garden. It's one of the newer astrantia varieties and definitely one of the best, thanks to its bright pink flowers and particularly long-flowering season, often from May until September.

Like most astrantias, 'Roma' revels in damp soil and dappled shade, where it will soon beef up into quite a substantial clump. It'll make excellent ground cover if planted in numbers at the edge of a woodland area, or to skirt around tall shrubs at the front of a shady border.

This astrantia seeds prolifically, although be warned that the seedlings may not come true to type. So the best way to increase this variety is to divide established clumps in spring, just as new growth begins.

TIP
Deadhead the old flowers throughout summer to keep the plant neat and to prevent excessive self-seeding.

Begonia
Begonia 'Apricot Shades'

Winning rosettes for shady containers

Time to plant: summer
Perennial H: 30cm (12in), S: 45cm (18in)

Flamboyant rosettes in sunny apricot and golden shades bring an added radiance to this trailing begonia right through the summer. Like all begonias, it loves a little shade and has an almost ceaseless energy that ensures it carries on blooming until the first frosts.

If you've been disappointed in the past with hanging baskets in the shade, try this begonia, or indeed any of the tuberous varieties. Instead of choosing those with dark red blooms, which tend to blend into the shadows, try varieties like this with pale lemons and gold blooms – they virtually beam out from a shady spot.

Young plants can be raised from seed, but 'Apricot Shades' is extremely small and can be a little tricky to germinate. It is so much easier when bought, and is ready to start flowering almost as soon as it is planted out in early summer.

TIP
Pale blue lobelia is lovely with this begonia as it will gently weave among the golden flowers, and it too likes a little shade.

Cluster-flowered bellflower
Campanula glomerata 'Bellefleur Blue'

Jewel clusters provide summer decoration

Time to plant: all year round
Perennial H: 10–45cm (4–18in), S: indefinite

Held extravagantly aloft on top of leafy stems like a cluster of blue sapphires, the flowers of this campanula always come as a pleasant surprise in summer. A cool border in partial shade is cultural bliss to this reliable perennial, where it will soon spread to form a large patch.

The self-supporting stems reach to about knee-height, so it's perfect placed near the front of a border. One of the loveliest ways to use its natural, spreading habit is to let it skirt around the bases of old-fashioned roses, which flower at the same time.

Once it gets established this bellflower needs little aftercare; a quick tidy up of old stems and leaves once they die back in the autumn is just about all you'll need do to keep it in tip-top condition.

TIP
Snip off the main flower cluster once the blooms start to fade and you'll often encourage a smaller second flush straight afterwards.

Bleeding heart
Dicentra 'King of Hearts'

A trump card for a shady border

Time to plant: all year round
Perennial H: 45cm (18in), S: 45cm (18in)

This fairly new introduction to the bleeding heart family has already earned a reputation for its extremely long-flowering period; it flowers itself almost silly when given a cool, shady border – often from spring, all summer long, into autumn.

Dicentra 'King of Hearts' is more compact than the common bleeding heart, *D. spectablis*, and the neat, fern-like leaves over which the flowers nod on arching stems also make an attractive feature.

Almost any soil suits this bleeding heart, but it doesn't like cold, heavy clay, so add plenty of compost when planting if your garden soil is a bit sticky.

TIP
This dicentra keeps its vigour if dug up and divided every few years. Do this in early spring, just as new growth starts. Replant strong divisions straight away in compost-enriched soil.

Foxglove
Digitalis purpurea 'Candy Mountain'

Ring the changes with a new foxglove

Time to plant: autumn or spring
Perennial H:1.2m (4ft), S: 45cm (18in)

You may have to look twice to recognise these robust, tapering spires as foxgloves as this new variety is the first foxglove with upward-facing flowers that can be raised from seed. The effect in the garden is simply stunning and, like the wild foxglove, it too thrives in shade.

The upward-facing flowers are not the only element that is unusual – it also has extremely sturdy stems, which makes this foxglove especially dramatic when used en masse.

Seeds sown indoors very early in spring may flower the first year, but it's easier to sow them in trays or small pots outside in early summer, which will provide plenty of sturdy young plants for putting into their final spot during autumn. These will flower the following year.

TIP
Foxglove seeds need light to germinate, so just sow them on the surface of the compost and cover lightly with vermiculite.

Escallonia
Escallonia 'Red Robin'

A compact evergreen that's big on style

Time to plant: all year round
Shrub H: 90cm (3ft), S: 90cm (3ft)

It may look like any other escallonia, but this new variety has been selected for its particularly compact nature, making it ideal for smaller gardens. Its bright red flowers are produced right through summer and gain an added intensity because they are set against glossy foliage.

All escallonias are reliable shrubs, even in a shady border, and they are extremely good at withstanding coastal winds. Ordinary fertile soil suits them fine, but prepare the ground before planting by adding some garden compost and a handful of general fertiliser. In severely cold winters you may get a bit of die-back on the shoot tips of escallonias, but they should resprout again from lower down in spring.

This compact variety will make an excellent low-flowering hedge, and just needs a quick trim in late summer to keep it looking smart.

TIP
Keep newly planted escallonias well watered until they establish, as they dry out very quickly in hot weather.

Fuchsia
Fuchsia 'Eva Boerg'

Dainty dancers on the summer stage

Time to plant: all year round
Shrub H: 30cm (12in), S: 45cm (18in)

A choreographed performance of perfectly turned out ballerinas lasts for months on the slender stems of this hardy fuchsia, the final encore often being as late as the first frosts in autumn. Unusually for a hardy fuchsia, the frilled flowers of 'Eva Boerg' are carried on spreading, almost trailing stems, which can make a very dramatic feature when they cascade over the sides of a large pot.

Although it will grow in sun, a little shade encourages a lush display because it helps to keep the roots cool, which fuchsias enjoy. All the stems are likely to look rather dead in winter – don't worry, just snip them back in spring when you see new shoots starting to emerge at the base. In cold areas, a generous mulch of leafy compost placed around the roots in autumn will provide a snug winter duvet.

TIP
Cuttings of all hardy fuchsias root extremely easily if taken in late summer. Pinch off any buds or flowers from the cuttings to divert their energy into rooting.

Fuchsia
Fuchsia 'Swingtime'

Up-tempo blooms for lively summer displays

Time to plant: summer
Shrub H: 30–60cm (12–24in),
S: 45–75cm (18–30in)

Voluptuously large flowers in a striking red and white combination ensure this popular variety has an honourable place in many summer containers. The catchy name reflects the energetic performance of blooms, which last until the autumn frosts.

All the bedding fuchsias like a bit of shade – especially during the hottest part of the day – and this also keeps the roots cool and stops them drying out. The trailing habit of 'Swingtime' makes it ideal for planting in hanging baskets or for tumbling over the edge of a large container.

Young plants can be planted outside after the risk of frost has passed in early summer.

TIP
Feed fuchsias regularly during summer to encourage even more of their flamboyant flowers.

Hardy cranesbill
Geranium 'Memories'

Small treasure for the front of a border

Time to plant: all year round
Perennial H: 15cm (6in), S: 30cm (12in)

This newly introduced hardy geranium forms a compact cushion of neatly lobed foliage, over which vivid, purplish-magenta flowers with dark centres are liberally sprinkled. These beautiful, tiny saucers are produced for months – from spring, right to the end of summer.

Geranium 'Memories' is perfect for the front of a border, rockery or even pots, and will happily tolerate light shade, especially if it gets sun for part of the day.

Provided it has reasonably fertile, well-drained soil, this pretty perennial is virtually trouble-free. It's also low maintenance; just quickly snip off the old leaves in late autumn when doing a pre-winter tidy up.

TIP
The hardy geranium family also contains a few types that will grow in quite deep shade. Look out for *G. macrorrhizum*, *G. nodosum* and *G. phaeum*, which are all easy to grow and make excellent ground cover.

Daylily
Hemerocallis 'Golden Chimes'

Let golden trumpets announce the start of summer

Time to plant: all year round
Perennial H: 90cm (3ft), 45cm (18in)

The dark mahogany-red buds of this daylily flare open into the most intense buttercup-yellow trumpets for many weeks over summer. 'Golden Chimes' is one of the more traditional varieties of the colourful daylily family, but it still has lots more style and grace than many of the newer introductions. And it also thrives in a bit of shade.

Like all daylilies the individual flowers only last a day, but there are plenty of plump buds ready and waiting to ensure a continuous show. Once the plant has flowered you can also look forward to extra autumn colour when all the strappy leaves are tinted with ochre and old gold.

Soil that doesn't dry out too much in summer will bring out the best from this easily grown perennial. It's lovely when used as a large drift and, because it comes into leaf early, it acts as a good, weed-suppressing ground cover for most of the year.

TIP
Rejuvenate mature plants every few years by dividing in autumn or early spring. Replant strong pieces in compost-enriched soil.

Hosta
Hosta 'Liberty'

A dramatic hosta to beat gloom and slugs

Time to plant: all year round
Perennial H: 75cm (30in), S: 90cm (3ft)

Variegated hostas like this new variety are simply indispensable if you have a shady garden. Their brightly edged leaves glint out from the darkest border, and the whole plant makes a bold statement all through the growing season.

The leaf edge of 'Liberty' starts a golden colour and then fades to striking white. The texture is also much thicker than many other varieties, and, as a result, it gets very little damage from all but the most sharply toothed slugs.

Their foliage is so dramatic that it's easy to forget that hostas have quite nice flowers too. 'Liberty' has particularly handsome lavender-purple bells that nod gracefully from its stout flower stems in summer. It also makes a superb feature in a large container, especially a brightly glazed terracotta pot.

TIP
Plant snowdrops around the base of the plant for a bit of extra colour before the hosta leaves unfurl.

Hydrangea
Hydrangea macrophylla

Winning heads with lasting style

Time to plant: all year round
Shrub H: 2m (6ft), S: 2.4m (8ft)

Your granny may have grown them, but hydrangeas have never really gone out of fashion – they are simply too valuable for their gloriously outrageous, colourful blooms. And they do so well in shade – even under trees.

There are basically two types of *Hydrangea macrophylla*: the mopheads and the lacecaps. Mopheads have flowers shaped like footballs, while lacecaps are daintier and only have a ring of colourful petals. Amongst these groups there are dozens of hydrangeas to choose from, including some new varieties with double flowers for an extra bit of swagger.

In addition to their flower size, it's the amazingly long season of colour that sets hydrangeas apart from many other shrubs. The flowers start to appear in summer and go through a fusion of shades (especially the mopheads), before bowing out in a blend of glowing crimsons, purple and russets in late autumn.

TIP
For the richest blue flowers hydrangeas need acid soil in the garden, otherwise grow a blue-flowered variety in a pot of ericaceous compost and apply a hydrangea blueing agent during summer.

Hydrangea
Hydrangea paniculata 'Burgundy Lace'

Late flush of colour

Time to plant: all year round
Shrub H: 3–7m (10–22ft), S: 2.4m (8ft)

Opening green then developing into a pristine white, the large conical heads of 'Burgundy Lace' only live up to its variety name as summer wanes, when dark claret and mauve shades seep into the petals. This plant will provide months of excitement in a large border and will happily grow in the dappled shade under trees.

To encourage strong, vigorous stems that will carry extra large flowerheads later in the year, prune all the stems almost to ground level in spring. If you prefer smaller but more numerous flowers, just give the plant a light prune in spring.

This hydrangea responds well to generous feeding and mulching every spring, especially if you are cutting it back for large flowers.

TIP
Leave on the old, papery flowerheads in winter as they look lovely when rimed with frost.

New Guinea busy Lizzie
Impatiens New Guinea Group 'Octavia'

Glam up outdoor containers

Time to plant: summer
Perennials H: 35cm (14in), S: 30cm (12in)

Larger and more dramatic than the usual bedding busy Lizzies, these New Guinea varieties show off their extravagant blooms over gorgeous bronzy, variegated or lush green foliage. When originally introduced they were treated just as indoor plants, but these striking plants will bring instant glamour to outdoor pots in summer.

Like the ordinary busy Lizzie, the New Guinea varieties thrive in cool shade, but what they really hate is overwatering – so go easy with the hose and let them dry out a little before giving them another drink. They also do best when sheltered from strong winds as this can scorch the large foliage.

TIP
Pick off the old blooms regularly to prevent them going mouldy in wet weather. This also keeps the display looking pristine and encourages more flowers.

Busy Lizzie
Impatiens walleriana

Bright solution for deep shade

Time to plant: summer
Perennial, but grown as annual
H: 60cm (2ft), S: 60cm (2ft)

Although many bedding plants love to bask in the sun, all busy Lizzies luxuriate in a shadier position. Some of their colours are ravishing, too, and include vivid Barbie pink, intense magenta and darkest crimson. The blush white and soft coral colours, however, look most effective in shade, sometimes appearing almost luminous.

Plants can be grown from seed and should be sown indoors in early spring. If only a few plants are needed it's usually best to buy these in flower in early summer, when it's safe to plant them out. One of the great advantages of busy Lizzies is that they never need deadheading; the old blooms simply fall off and are replaced by the ongoing surge of blooms that last right into autumn.

Cuttings root very easily in summer – even in a glass of water on the windowsill. Once the roots establish, these cuttings can be potted up and kept over winter as houseplants.

TIP
If you are growing busy Lizzies in containers, mix water-retaining granules into the compost to keep it moist.

Welsh poppy
Meconopsis cambrica

Go native with citrus shades

Time to plant: all year round
Perennial H: 45cm (18in), S: 25cm (10in)

The meconopsis family contains the much-coveted blue Himalayan poppies, but this native perennial is no less valuable for its bright lemon or zesty orange saucers that gleam out from a shady area right through summer and autumn. It spreads freely by self-seeding (some may say too freely) but, in the right spot, such as a woodland garden or when softening the edge of a very shady gravel path, it's simply unbeatable.

You are more likely to find seed rather than plants of Welsh poppies at the garden centre, but the seeds germinate easily if sown in pots outside during spring, which can then be transplanted to their final homes in summer. Look out for a double-flowered variety called *M. c.* var. *aurantiaca flore-pleno* – it's rather a mouthful but it's a charming plant that comes true from seed. The frilly rosette-shaped flowers create a lovely cottage-garden effect.

TIP
Sow the fine seeds thinly on the surface of the compost, just covering them with a sprinkling of sand or vermiculite.

Blue Himalayan Poppy
Meconopsis 'Willie Duncan'

Rich blooms for cool shade

Time to plant: all year round
Perennial H: 90cm (3ft), S: 45cm (18in)

The glamour models of any shady garden in summer are the Himalayan blue poppies, with flowers so intensely blue they could be sculpted from the finest lapis lazuli. The final wow is the gorgeous cluster of golden stamens in the centre of each flower, cradled by a swirl of satiny petals.

All Himalayan blue poppies are worthy of a spot in your garden, but you may find some named varieties, such as the exquisite 'Willie Duncan', have a particular intensity of blue.

One thing they all have in common is their love of moisture-retentive soil, especially in summer. Mulching the soil with compost every year in spring works wonders to help seal in summer moisture. Ideally, the soil should also be slightly acid too, but you can grow them in most areas by adding plenty of ericaceous compost.

TIP
Take precautions against slugs and snails, which will eat the young foliage in spring.

Nemesia
Nemesia 'Berries and Cream'

New nemesia for an eye-catching display

Time to plant: summer
Annual 20cm (8in), S: 15cm (6in)

New varieties of nemesia are making their mark, thanks to a long and profuse flowering season. This fancy two-toned variety is particularly eye-catching, with blackberry-and-creamy-white flowers enhanced by a golden centre. It does well in a little shade and makes a refreshing change from the usual bedding plants, such as pansies and busy Lizzies, which also tolerate low light levels.

In addition to its prolific flowering, this variety has been selected for its compact habit, and it makes a wonderful display in a container or as an edging plant. Get close enough to its flowers and you'll also discover that it's very sweetly scented.

There's no real need to deadhead old blooms as new flowers will automatically keep opening through summer.

TIP
Although nemesia is best treated as an annual, cuttings can be rooted in summer and overwintered in a frost-free greenhouse.

Tobacco plant
Nicotiana sylvestris

Add natural scent to summer evenings

Time to plant: summer
Annual H: 1.5m (5ft), S: 60cm (2ft)

A giant among tobacco plants, *Nicotiana sylvestris* rockets up to nearly head height, revealing whorls of elegant, long-tubed white flowers in summer. As temperatures dip in the evening, these gently nodding flowers fill the air with a glorious, exotic perfume.

The tobacco plant is a natural, shade-loving plant (in fact the word *sylvestris* means from the woods), and its large, white flowers ensure it stands out well from the shadows.

Unlike bedding nicotianas, which are readily available as plants in summer, this one is usually only available as seed, but it's very easy to grow. Sow the seed indoors during spring and transplant out young plants in early summer for a display the same year. Although often grown as an annual, plants may overwinter outside in mild areas.

TIP
Grow a few extra plants in big pots to use as fillers for any gaps in the summer border.

Giant cowslip
Primula florindae

Add spectacular light and scent to shady spots

Time to plant: all year round
Perennial H: 1.2m (4ft), S: 90cm (3ft)

This beefy Himalayan relative of our native cowslip puts its own stylish stamp on the summer garden, as whorls of lemon-sherbet flowers stretch past its lush leaves. Nuzzle your nose into these nodding bells and you'll find that they are drenched in the most refreshing, lemony scent. The pale yellow flowers have an almost luminous quality and shine out from the gloom of a shady border.

Moisture is the secret to getting the best from this characterful perennial – it really wants to have its feet in permanently squelchy soil. The giant cowslip will flourish in the damp ground beside a pond or in a bog garden, and in fact it looks very much at home anywhere beside water.

Once established you'll often find self-sown seedlings appear around your plant; these can be left to increase your colony or transplanted to another spot in the garden.

TIP
The pale lemon bells look fantastic alongside the jagged-edged purple leaves of an ornamental rhubarb, such as *Rheum palmatum* 'Atrosanguineum'.

Rhododendron
Rhododendron 'Ernest Inman'

Show-stopping rhododendrons

Time to plant: all year round
Shrub H: 2m (6½ft), S: 2m (6½ft)

For sheer floral flamboyancy, rhododendrons have few equals in the early summer garden. This is one of the dwarf *Rhododendron yakushimanum* hybrids, and will only grow to about waist high and fits easily into a small garden. It loves being tucked in a bit of shade and will cheerfully grow under the branches of tall trees or in a border that only gets sunlight for part of the day.

Like most rhododendrons, 'Ernest Inman' prefers acid soil, but don't worry if your garden hasn't got any as it's compact enough to grow in a large tub of ericaceous (lime-free) compost. Its evergreen leaves are a joy throughout the year, especially when the new shuttlecocks of foliage unfurl in summer just after the spectacular fistfuls of flowers.

TIP
Remove old flowerheads carefully because young shoots are positioned just behind them.

Rodgersia
Rodgersia aesculifolia

Give summer foliage displays a bronzed look

Time to plant: all year round
Perennial H: 2m (6½ft), S: 1m (3½ft)

Rugged good looks are a natural feature of this superb plant, which forms clumps of splayed, jagged foliage. These gorgeous, textured leaves usually emerge bronze before turning green, and then assume warm tints again in autumn.

This perennial is very much at home in a shady border and does especially well when the soil doesn't dry out too much in summer. In addition to the handsome leaves, you can expect stems of frothy white flowers in summer.

Once established, rodgersias need very little care, apart from cutting down the old leaves in late autumn. New plants can be obtained by digging up an established clump in early spring and cutting off sections from the edge that have a bud and some roots. Replant these immediately in compost-enriched soil and water them in dry spells until established.

TIP
Plant rodgersias in a large group to provide excellent ground cover in damp soil.

Fairy fan-flower
Scaevola aemula

Keep containers colourful all summer long

Time to plant: summer
Perennial H: 50cm (20in), S: 50cm (20in)

The fairy fan-flower is a relative newcomer among summer bedding plants, but it has quickly earned a reputation for its fantastic long and prolific flowering, even in a little shade. The individual flowers, shaped like dainty, delft-blue fans, open throughout the entire summer along its trailing stems.

The vigorous trailing habit of fairy fan-flower means that it is mostly used in hanging baskets or large containers, where it will quickly make glorious cascades of blue flowers. Regular liquid feeding in summer and attention to watering in dry spells will ensure the most spectacular display.

Fairy fan-flower makes a wonderful under-storey to a large, upright fuchsia or standard marguerite daisy.

TIP
The fairy fan-flower can become a little straggly, so pinch back long stems when planting to promote a well-branched plant.

Viburnum
Viburnum sargentii 'Onondaga'

A stunning shrub for all seasons

Time to plant: all year round
Shrub H: 3m (10ft), S: 2m (6½ft)

With impeccable style and colour coordination, this choice viburnum makes a long, lively contribution to the garden. Its maple-like leaves, burnished bronze-red when young, are the perfect background for the swirls of white lacecap flowers that surround the dark red centres.

The flowers, which last for a good few weeks in summer, are eventually replaced by clusters of red berries that persist well into autumn. At this stage the leaves assume a vibrant, reddish-purple glow. As with virtually its entire family, *Viburnum sargentii* 'Onondaga' will happily grow in a little shade, and because it can stretch to about head height, it's ideal for the back of a large border. You can keep it a little more compact by pruning back some of the shoots after flowering.

TIP
Young plants can be easily raised from cuttings, selected from healthy young shoots in summer.

Heartsease
Viola tricolor

A delicious summer beauty

Time to plant: spring
Annual H: 8–12cm (3½–4½in), S: 10–15cm
(4–6in)

Parent to the large-flowered pansy, this
dainty viola is a captivating beauty when its
prettily patterned blooms unfurl in summer.
You may, however, find flowers peeping out
at you virtually throughout the year, and
their dainty faces are adorable as the
weather turns chilly in autumn or at the
first sign of spring.

Individual plants can sometimes survive
for a few years, but *Viola tricolor* is mostly
an annual that self-seeds freely once
established. To grow heartsease, the seeds
can be sown directly in the ground in
spring or in small pots which can be later
transplanted to their final position. It looks
lovely in a wild garden or skirting around
the bare legs of roses.

The heartsease is a native plant that
thrives in quite poor soil, and will happily
tolerate a bit of shade for part of the day.

TIP
For a dash of colour in a summer salad,
sprinkle over a few of its edible flowers.

Pansy
Viola x *wittrockiana* 'Chianti'

Velvety blooms for instant colour

Time to plant: spring or autumn
Perennial, but grown as annual or biennial
H: 15–23cm (6–9in), S: 23–30cm (9–12in)

Jolly-faced pansies never fail to lift the spirits. Their large, velvety flowers are especially useful in containers as they provide such an immediate effect and, thanks to the vast range of varieties available, they provide a wonderful opportunity to create amazing colour-coordinated plant combinations. Best of all, they just love to grow in a little shade.

This new variety with pretty, ruffled flowers, can be summer- or winter-flowering, depending on whether you sow the seed in early spring or summer – early sowings will flower the same year. Pansies are best sown in a seed tray on the windowsill or in a glasshouse, and transplanted later into the garden or containers.

Although pansies can last for more than one year, they often get straggly, so they are best replaced with fresh, new plants each season.

TIP
To encourage the longest display of flowers, pinch off the old flowers, stem and all, as soon as they fade. This prevents the plant setting seed and diverts energy into more blooms.

Weigela
Weigela 'Monet'

Update the old favourites

Time to plant: all year round
Shrub H: 90cm (3ft), S: 90cm (3ft)

This new introduction is a snazzy addition to the weigela family. Its crisply margined foliage is beautifully blushed with pink at the tips right through the growing season, and this helps it to cut a dash, even in a little bit of shade. You can expect an extra treat in early summer, when purplish-pink trumpets flare out amongst the foliage.

Another useful merit of this exciting variety is its extremely compact habit – rarely reaching 90cm (3ft) tall, even when fully grown. This makes it great for tiny gardens or even for growing in a large tub on the patio.

Like the entire weigela family, this new variety seems to thrive in almost any soil, so long as it's well drained. Because it's naturally compact, no regular pruning is required.

TIP
Its combination of hardiness and dense, compact habit makes it ideal for growing in a very windy garden.

Japanese maple
Acer palmatum

See summer out in a blaze of glory

Time to plant: all year round
Tree H: 7.5m (25ft), S: 9m (30ft)

From the moment its neatly folded leaves unfold in spring, you know a Japanese maple has been hiding something special. These new leaves gradually expand into delicately lobed blades suffused with a variety of shades from green and gold to the most sumptuous dark purple. Come late autumn, there's another treat when fiery tints whoosh through the compact canopy.

Japanese maples thrive in dappled shade and are much easier to grow than many people imagine. A little shelter is beneficial to protect them from cold winds in spring, in particular, which can scorch newly emerging leaves. Any fertile, well-drained soil is suitable – if it's on the acid side, all the better, but that isn't essential.

There are many varieties of Japanese maple and some of the more compact types, such as *Acer palmatum* 'Dissectum', do extremely well in pots, instantly bringing a touch of Oriental elegance to the garden.

TIP
Japanese maples hate to be planted deeply – the top of the compost in the pot should be level with the surface of the soil in the garden after planting out.

Japanese maple
Acer palmatum var. *dissectum* 'Baldsmith'

Let lacy leaves sizzle in autumn

Time to plant: all year round
Tree H: 1.8m (6ft), S: 1.8m (6ft)

Lacy-leaved Japanese maples always turn heads in a garden, especially when they have matured into a gorgeous specimen that looks a bit like a venerable bonsai. Even after decades of growth these compact maples may still be only waist high, but they will have grown into the most characterful, sweeping shapes.

There are quite a few Japanese maples with dissected foliage; some are green in summer, others are shades of matt red or purple. This, however, is merely their summer attire; once the first chilly nights of autumn arrive their lacy leaves flare into fiery orange, yellow and red.

Because of their compact size, lacy-leaved Japanese maples are ideally suited to growing in pots and are happy to tolerate a bit of shade, too. Choose a soil-based compost for ease of watering and because it has more substance than the peat-based kind.

TIP
Position this Japanese maple away from cold winds, which can cause leaf scorch, especially when the new foliage unfurls in spring.

Japanese anemone
Anemone x *hybrida* 'Géante des Blanches'

Swirls of light in dark autumn days

Time to plant: all year round
Perennial H: 1.2–1.5m (4–5ft), S: indefinite

The pristine, semi-double swirls of this Japanese anemone almost leap out from a shady border as the light begins to dwindle in early autumn. Although it can reach up to 1.5m (5ft) high, the long, wiry stems of *Anemone* x *hybrida* 'Géante des Blanches' never need staking. It's perfect for lighting the gloom beneath dense, overhanging trees.

You may find that if Japanese anemones like your garden, they will very soon make a bid for a takeover. That's fine under trees or in difficult places, but they can soon colonize a border and spread in between other plants, so plant them in places where they have room to roam. All anemones thrive in ordinary soil, provided it is well drained.

In addition to this white form, there are plenty of pink varieties of Japanese anemone, including 'Pamina', which has deep purplish-pink, semi-double flowers on compact stems.

TIP
If growing Japanese anemones beneath trees, underplant the area with bluebells, which will be in flower as the anemone leaves emerge, so providing another season of colour.

Cotoneaster
Cotoneaster splendens

Berry splendour for autumn

Time to plant: all year round
Shrub H: 2m (6½ft), S: 2.4m (8ft)

Many berrying plants are suitable for shady areas, but few of them can compete with the cotoneasters for sheer exuberance and versatility. Among the family you can find types for ground cover, small trees, hedges and even walls. They are also tremendously easy to grow in almost any position.

This Chinese species, *Cotoneaster splendens*, makes a very elegant, arching shrub that is laden with flame-red berries in autumn. The blush-pink flowers in spring are also an attractive feature and become a magnet for bees, which love them for their rich nectar. This plant eventually grows to about head height, so it is ideal for a large border, but try to place it where its arching stems can be seen to full benefit.

It needs no special attention to keep it happy, but you can still give it a treat every spring by scattering a handful of general fertiliser around its base.

TIP
For extra summer colour, plant the flame creeper (*Tropaeolum speciosum*) nearby so that it can reach into the cotoneaster and drape it with swags of red flowers.

Hardy cyclamen
Cyclamen hederifolium

Petite bulb for a late floral treat

Time to plant: early autumn
Perennial H: 10–13cm (4–5in), S: 15cm (6in)

A volley of tiny shuttlecocks shooting just above the ground in early autumn is the unmistakable hallmark of this reliable bulb. It's perfectly adapted to growing under trees as it has a summer rest while the trees are in full leaf and only starts to stir again once the first tweedy-brown shades appear in the canopy.

Dressed in shades of sugary pink and glistening white, the flowers of *Cyclamen hederifolium* form gorgeous pools of colour just before their leaves emerge – they are also pretty dapper and reveal exquisite silver patterns on each ivy-shaped blade. Because the leaves remain evergreen through the winter, they can be used as an ideal background to snowdrops and other early bulbs.

Once established this hardy cyclamen spreads by self-seeding, helped by ants that gather the seeds for their sugary coating and unwittingly spread them about the garden.

TIP
Buy dry tubers in early autumn and plant them out immediately, nestling them just below the soil surface.

Pineapple flower
Eucomis comosa 'Sparkling Burgundy'

Add a tropical twist to an autumnal garden

Time to plant: spring
Perennial H: 75cm (30in), S: 20cm (8in)

Aptly named the pineapple flower, this South African bulb brings a slice of the tropics to the late summer and autumn garden with its cylindrical spikes of starry flowers, topped with a tuft of foliage. Its lush, maroon-suffused leaves are all the better for a little shade, and it grows best in soil that doesn't dry out too much in summer.

Eucomis bulbs should be planted about 10cm (4in) deep in spring, or you can plant out pot-grown plants at virtually any time of year. It looks fantastic in a large, glazed pot on the patio and will be happy for quite a few years without any special care. Old, established clumps will benefit from being carefully dug up and divided in spring.

TIP
Leave on the old seedheads through the winter as they look gorgeous decorated with dewy cobwebs or glistening with frost.

Japanese aralia
Fatsia japonica

A big statement for small gardens

Time to plant: all year round
Shrub H: 1.5–4m (5–13ft), S: 1.5–4m (5–13ft)

One of the most dramatic shrubs for shade, this exotic-leaved evergreen looks like it should be cosseted in a conservatory. It is, however, completely hardy in most areas outside and will eventually make a magnificent, large, very exciting specimen. Fatsias have a further treat in store during autumn, when branched heads of drumstick-like white flowers crown each stem.

Any well-drained soil that doesn't become too dry in summer suits this leafy giant. It can grow up to 4m (13ft) tall when fully grown, but you can keep it to a more manageable size by pruning the stems back a little each spring.

TIP
Large-leaved architectural plants, such as this fatsia, look spectacular in a small town garden, and can actually make such a space appear bigger.

Snowdrop
Galanthus reginae-olgae

Autumn flowers on a winter favourite

Time to plant: late autumn
Perennial H: 10cm (4in), S: 5cm (2in)

Snowdrops are often planted under trees because they flower in the depths of winter and then die down again before the tree canopy fills in overhead. *Galanthus reginae-olgae* is a little different because it begins flowering in autumn, providing a little sneak preview of what's in store from the rest of the family in the New Year.

Although it's not as vigorous as the common snowdrop (*G. nivalis*) this unusual species enjoys a similar spot in the garden, such as beneath deciduous trees. It can also be grown very successfully in a terracotta pot, being kept in a cold frame or unheated glasshouse. If you get close enough to the blooms you may even detect its surprisingly sweet fragrance.

Over a few years this snowdrop gradually increases into a little clump, which can be lifted and divided after flowering. Do this while the plants are still in leaf, just like the ordinary types.

TIP
It's best to buy plants in pots rather than bulbs, which are often so dried-out that they fail to grow after planting.

Willow gentian
Gentiana asclepiadea

Break up autumnal hues with blasts of blue

Time to plant: all year round
Perennial H: 60–90cm (2–3ft), S: 45cm (18in)

Blue is a very welcome colour in the early autumn garden just as many leaves start turning brown, and gentians are masters of this treasured colour. Many gentians are small alpines, but the arching wands of the willow gentian will easily reach about 60-90cm (2-3ft), so it's ideal for using in a border among other perennials.

Its willowy stems, clasping the sapphire trumpets, look magical arching out among ferns, hostas and the low, yellow-tinged leaves of the Japanese grass *Hakonechloa macra* 'Aureola'. Position this gentian where there's room for its stems to arch out naturally – the edge of a pathway or on a raised bed, for instance.

Gentiana asclepiadea prefers a cool, shady position, such as an east-facing border or a place under a light canopy of trees. It's not that fussy about soil, though, provided it is enriched with plenty of compost and doesn't dry out too much in summer.

TIP
Once established, this gentian does best when left undisturbed and lasts for many years without needing any attention.

Lords and ladies
Arum italicum subsp. *italicum* 'Marmoratum'

A silver lining under dark winter clouds

Time to plant: autumn
Perennial H: 30cm (12in), S: 15cm (6in)

An aristocratic relative of our native lords and ladies, this arum has beautiful, arrow-shaped leaves shot through with a tracery of silver veins. It's particularly suited for growing under trees, because its fresh leaves emerge in autumn, just as the tree canopy above is thinking about calling it a day.

The gorgeous, waxy leaves of 'Marmoratum' remain right through winter and spring, before dying down for a summer rest. The greeny-white flowers that appear among the leaves in spring are not especially colourful, but are replaced by heads of showy red berries that persist into autumn.

The dry bulbs, which are actually tubers, can be planted in early autumn or you can buy pot-grown plants that can be planted any time.

TIP
The leaves and berries are ideal in winter flower arrangements.

Spotted laurel
Aucuba japonica 'Picturata'

A plant that's pure gold for every shady spot

Time to plant: all year round
Shrub H: 3m (10ft), S: 3m (10ft)

An almost indestructible nature, combined with handsome, evergreen foliage, makes the spotted laurel one of the very best shrubs to grow in a shady garden. It will even tolerate dry shade under trees, and is particularly useful in town gardens where traffic pollution can be a problem.

Most aucuba varieties have gold-speckled leaves, which bring flickers of brightness to a dark area all through the year, but they are especially lovely in the depths of winter. As an extra bonus, female varieties, such as 'Crotonifolia', produce quite large red berries that colour up in winter.
To make sure you get these berries, plant with a male variety such as 'Picturata' or 'Golden King' nearby to pollinate the female flowers. No regular care is needed once they are established, but plants can be pruned in spring if necessary.

TIP
Aucubas make a lovely alternative hedge in a town garden, and can be kept neat by clipping back a little once a year.

Common box
Buxus sempervirens

Let box cut a swathe through the winter garden

Time to plant: all year round
Shrub H: 5m (16½ft), S: 5m (16½ft)

Clipped into strong, geometric shapes, such as spheres and pyramids, box plants can become living architectural pieces that help link the house and garden. The common box (*Buxus sempervirens*) is a remarkably adaptable evergreen and will thrive in quite dense shade. It's also very easy to grow in any well-drained soil or large pots filled with soil-based compost.

To maintain a crisp outline on box topiary, clip it at least once or twice a year during the summer. A pair of sheep shears or small hedge clippers is ideal. Old neglected box plants will also respond well to hard pruning in the spring.

Variegated varieties of box, such as *B. s.* 'Marginata', and 'Latifolia Maculata', are all excellent in deep shade. A shorter variety, called 'Suffruticosa', is best for creating low edging along a path.

TIP
Feed pot-grown box with a slow-release fertiliser in spring. This will keep the leaves rich green for the rest of the year.

Mezereon
Daphne mezereum

Create a perfume trail around your winter garden

Time to plant: all year round
Shrub H: 1.2m (4ft), S: 1m (3½ft)

In the first chilly weeks of the New Year, the bare stems of this daphne become encrusted with the most deliciously scented pink flowers. One sniff is rarely enough from these flower-packed stems, which have the kind of exotic perfume you'd expect to find from a far more tropical flower.

Unlike some daphnes, *Daphne mezereum* is pretty easy to grow in most soils, especially if they are on the limy side, and it also loves a little bit of shade.

Red berries appear on the stems after flowering, and these can be used to raise new plants. Collect them as soon as they are ripe, wash off the outer red coats and sow them in pots of compost. Place them outside and you will find small seedlings emerging in a few months. You may have to wait a few years for them to flower, but it'll be worthwhile when their first flowers start to open.

TIP
Young plants establish best. Don't transplant daphnes once established as they hate to be moved.

Winter aconite
Eranthis hyemalis Tubergenii Group 'Guinea Gold'

Create a blanket of gold with this winter warmer

Time to plant: autumn
Perennial H: 8–10cm (3½–4in), S: 5cm (2in)

A ruff of frilled leaves makes the fresh-faced, golden flowers of the winter aconite appear like a gathering of tiny choirboys as they emerge from the chilly February soil. The plant thrives in the bare soil beneath trees and eventually spreads out, forming the most magical blanket of gold.

This variety is a selected form of the winter aconite, which has slightly larger flowers, but the ordinary *Eranthis hyemalis* is the one to choose if you want a plant that will spread and create large colonies. The unusual-shaped tubers, which look a bit like a very tiny dahlia tuber, are available in autumn, and it's a good idea to soak them for a day before planting as they are often a little dried out.

Winter aconites thrive in most soils, but they seem to do best if the soil is slightly limy.

TIP
Winter aconites are perfect companions to snowdrops and *Cyclamen coum*, which together form a colourful tapestry in late winter.

Lenten rose
Helleborus x *hybridus*

A colourful nod to winter

Time to plant: all year round
Perennial H: 45cm (18in), S: 45cm (18in)

Sumptuous nodding saucers, in a range of seductive colours, open on this invaluable perennial throughout the depths of winter. From ivory-white and yellow through to pink, plum and even sloe black, you won't be able to resist tilting the flower heads upwards to see a freckling of darker spots.

Helleborus x *hybridus* loves a cool, shady border, especially in soil that remains cool and damp during summer. A deep mulch of garden compost will retain moisture on drier soils and help to suppress weeds.

This hellebore can be planted in the garden almost any time of year, but it's a good idea to choose your plant when it's in flower so you can select your favourite colour. This can be trickier than it sounds when faced with umpteen colours that all look simply gorgeous!

TIP
To reduce the chance of an overwintering fungal disease affecting the new foliage, remove all old leaves in winter before the flowers start to appear. You'll also be able to see the flowers better.

Stinking iris
Iris foetidissima

Seedheads provide a winter cracker

Time to plant: all year round
Perennial H: 30–90cm (1–3ft), S: indefinite

Rather unfairly, this plant is known as the stinking iris because its leaves have a pungent aroma if crushed. If you don't go out of your way to bruise a leaf, this evergreen iris has much to offer, especially to the winter garden.

As irises go, the flowers of *Iris foetidissima* are quite subtle and appear during early summer in an unusual blend of muted purple and yellow. The seedpods that follow, however, have plenty of panache when they split open to reveal rows of scarlet seeds. Somehow these seeds manage to cling on for most of winter and glow like miniature embers, especially in frosty weather.

This iris thrives in the deep shade under trees or at the base of evergreen hedges, and can tolerate very poor, dry soil. Look out for its variegated variety, which adds an extra dash of colour to a shady border.

TIP
Snip off a few seedpods to add an unusual twist to a Christmas wreath.

Honesty
Lunaria annua

Light up the winter garden with silver moons

Time to plant: autumn
Biennial H: 90cm (3ft), S: 30cm (12in)

The branched heads of purple or white flowers in late spring on this biennial are really just the warm-up act for its amazing, silvery seedheads. The individual round seedpods are quite dull at first, but as they split open in autumn to release the seeds they reveal a translucent, silvery panel in the centre that persists all winter. Honesty is absolutely magical under trees where low winter sunshine reaches in to illuminate its tiny, silver moons.

Any shady spot is perfect for growing honesty, and it's very easy to raise from seed sown in pots and placed outside in summer. The fairly large seeds are easy to handle and can be sown individually in small pots that can be potted on later and then planted out in autumn. At that stage you should have strong, bushy plants that will flower profusely the following spring and early summer.

TIP
Get maximum colour in a small space by underplanting honesty with tulips, which will flower at the same time.

Mahonia
Mahonia japonica

Fill the winter garden with gentle fragrance

Time to plant: all year round
Shrub H: 2m (6½ft), S: 3m (10ft)

Even in the deepest shade this evergreen shrub manages to turn on the charm. The magnificent, glossy leaves, hugely architectural throughout the year, are crowned with sprays of yellow flowers during the shortest days of autumn and winter. If you risk getting among its prickly leaves to have a sniff at these flowers, you'll be rewarded with a delicious waft of lily-of-the-valley fragrance.

Like its spiny, leathery leaves, this shrub is pretty tough and survives even in poor soil, provided it's well drained. It grows particularly well under large trees and in shady town gardens. You'll probably find the more popular *Mahonia* x *media* 'Charity' at the garden centre, which is a good alternative.

TIP
Old, leggy plants respond very well to a hard chop down in early spring and will shoot again even from bare stems. Encourage a quick recovery by feeding and mulching around the base.

Primrose
Primula

Brightly coloured perennials for containers and the garden

Time to plant: autumn
Perennial H: 10cm (4in), S: 10cm (4in)

Bedding primroses come to the rescue when gardens need a little bit of extrovert colour in the overcast days of late winter and early spring. The jolly blooms of these hybrids open in a range of colours that you'd expect to find in a sweet shop – from white to strawberry-pink, lemon-yellow, orange, red and even navy blue. The plants are normally starting to flower when you see them for sale in autumn, so you can choose exactly the shade you like for the most carefully colour-coordinated display.

Wherever they are planted in the garden primroses bring instant cheer, whether it's a few in a window box, a pot outside the door or a little patch of them in the border. They are, of course, perennials, like our native primrose, but the flower size tends to reduce in subsequent years, so these primroses should be replaced every year for the best results, especially if you are growing them in pots.

TIP
Pinch off the old blooms as they fade as wet weather can cause them to become mouldy, which can spread to unopened flower buds.

Christmas box

Sarcococca hookeriana var. *humilis*

A gift of scent during the festive season

Time to plant: all year round
Shrub H: 60cm (2ft), S: 1m (3½ft)

It may be discreet in flower, but the tiny white blooms of Christmas box show their extrovert side with their sweet fragrance, which generously laces the crisp air in late winter. A plant near a door will be a source of great pleasure for many weeks, whether it's planted in a nearby border or tucked into a container.

Apart from the flowers, the neat, dense, suckering habit of this evergreen is very useful in the garden as ground cover, especially in shade. Very little aftercare is required once it has established, but plants can be trimmed back straight after flowering, if required.

Damp, but not waterlogged, soil suits it best. A little feeding will prevent the leaves yellowing if it is in very poor soil, or if it has been growing for a few seasons in a pot.

TIP
Use this Christmas box to edge a border as a very fragrant alternative to common box (*Buxus sempervirens*).

Skimmia
Skimmia japonica subsp. *reevesiana*

Ruby-red berries for winter glamour

Time to plant: all year round
Shrub H: 7m (22ft), S: 90cm (3ft)

Clusters of bright, ruby-red berries usually ride out the winter intact on this compact variety, thanks to their weather-resistant, waxy coats. The long-lasting colour during the season of shortest days makes this skimmia ideal for bringing an extra sparkle to winter pots, or for cutting a dash at the front of a shady border.

Like all skimmias, it prefers slightly acid soil. Don't worry if your soil isn't acid, though, as it's easy to grow in containers filled with ericaceous compost. Try planting it up with a bronze phormium and orange pansies for a vivid flash of winter colour.

Skimmias usually have male and female flowers on separate plants, but this variety has both together, which means you only need one plant to produce plenty of berries.

TIP
To ensure the leaves stay a dark, lustrous green, feed this skimmia during the summer with a fertiliser made for ericaceous plants.

Hard fern
Blechnum spicant

Laddered leaves add an extra, quirky touch

Time to plant: all year round
Fern H: 20-50cm (8-20in), S: 60cm (2ft)

Ferns are synonymous with shade – they just adore life in the cool, moist soil under trees or in areas shielded from direct sunshine. The hard fern is actually a native British plant, but it is well worth cultivating in the garden because of its neatly laddered, evergreen fronds.

Blechnum spicant does best in lime-free soil, so add some ericaceous compost when planting if your soil is limy, or plant it in containers using the same compost. It loves to be in soil that stays wet, especially during summer, so mulch generously with garden compost or old leaf mould every year to conserve moisture in drier positions. Water pot-grown plants with rainwater, as tap water can be very limy.

TIP
Hard fern looks a treat in winter pots beside the ruby berries of a skimmia, and winter-flowering heathers.

Japanese boxwood
Buxus microphylla 'Golden Triumph'

Colourful edges make a brighter box

Time to plant: all year round
Shrub H: 75cm (2½ft), S: 1.5m (5ft)

A sharp edging of yellow on every leaf makes this new box variety glint through even the darkest shade. It has a naturally compact habit, only growing to about waist high when mature, so it's ideal for growing in pots. It would also make a brighter alternative to common box
(B. *sempervirens*) for edging in a shady garden.

Like ordinary box, Japanese boxwood needs to be fed well to be grown as a permanent container specimen, otherwise the leaves will become a rather sickly, bronzy-orange. Slow-release fertiliser granules are the easiest way of doing this, which are available as thimble-shaped clusters that can be simply pushed into the compost every spring to release nutrients over an entire growing season.

Cuttings of *Buxus microphylla* 'Golden Triumph' will root easily if taken in summer and placed in pots of compost. Stand these pots somewhere shady with a plastic bag over the top to increase humidity, and the cuttings should root in a few weeks.

TIP
If you want to train plants into a sphere or other large topiary shape, plant several small plants together for a quicker result.

Tree fern
Dicksonia antartica

Bring a taste of the tropics to a dull, shady spot

Time to plant: summer
Fern H: 6m (20ft), S: 4m (13ft)

Tree ferns have become a favourite plant for bringing a tropical theme to a garden, and you don't need a sunny spot to grow one, as they revel in shade.

These tree ferns are much hardier than once imagined, and will sail through most winters outside. In colder areas, or for an extra safeguard against a hard frost, you can tuck a few good handfuls of straw on top of the growing point, and hold it in place with some chicken wire. This will act as a snug blanket during hard winter weather, and can be removed in spring.

When buying your tree fern, choose a pot-grown plant that already has some clear stem showing; smaller ones can take a while to look like tree ferns. A place under established trees, where the tree fern will get both a little shelter and some shade, makes a perfect home. You can also grow tree ferns very easily in large pots and, being evergreen, they look great all through the year.

TIP
In summer, water the fibrous-looking stem of the tree fern, as well as the root area, as this is where the plant absorbs a lot of its moisture.

Japanese spindle
Euonymus japonicus 'Aureus'

A tough evergreen with a heart of gold

Time to plant: all year round
Shrub H: 1.5m (5ft), S: 1m (3½ft)

This is an invaluable shrub for coastal gardens where it is often used as a hedge to protect plants from salt-laden winds. Happy in shade, or indeed full sun, it has a useful knack of tolerating almost any soil, provided it is well drained.

Unlike the ground-covering varieties of euonymus, this one can stretch to head height and is ideal for the back of the border. You do need to keep an eye out for mildew during summer, though, which will be visible as a powdery white coating on the leaves. Plants that get too dry are more prone to this fungal disease, so mulch generously around the base of the plant with garden compost in spring to conserve moisture.

Cuttings are easy to root in summer, and any extra young plants you grow this way are ideal for tucking into winter pots for a splash of green and gold.

TIP
Plain green shoots can often appear on the plant, and these should be snipped off straight away to prevent the plant reverting back to all-green.

Holly
Ilex aquifolium 'Myrtifolia Aurea'

Golden leaves that pierce through the shade

Time to plant: all year round
Shrub H: 3m (10ft), S: 1.8m (6ft)

Virtually all hollies will grow in a little shade, and this gold-variegated variety certainly makes a bright contribution throughout the year. The small, spiny leaves are held on gorgeous purple stems that form a very neat, pyramidal shrub. This compact nature makes it a very good specimen plant for a large container if you want to create an impressive feature on a shady patio or beside a doorway.

The colourful foliage and shapely habit of 'Myrtifolia Aurea' are reasons enough for growing it in your garden, but don't expect berries from it because, being male, it won't produce any. However, it will help pollinate your female varieties.

In the garden it'll grow in almost any well-drained soil, and is a trouble-free evergreen once established.

TIP
Use soil-based, multi-purpose compost if growing this holly in a container; this is easier to keep moist than peat-based compost and is also heavier, which makes the pot more stable.

Photinia
Photinia x *fraseri* 'Red Robin'

Filled with the colourful flush of youth

Time to plant: all year round
Shrub H: 5m (16ft), S: 5m (16ft)

Tipped with new copper-red shoots from early spring until autumn, this evergreen shrub brings a flicker of brightness to large beds almost throughout the entire year, even in a little shade. The red leaves will gradually turn glossy green, and are dense enough to make a good hedge to provide privacy or screening.

This photinia has also become popular as a clipped standard, especially for pots framing a doorway. Simply clip the foliage to produce a ball of leaves on top of a bare stem. If you feel nervous about doing this, topiarised plants are readily available, giving an instant effect although they can be quite expensive.

Soil-based compost is best when growing these plants in pots, and they are pretty easy to please in the garden, too, flourishing in most well-drained soils.

TIP
Regular pruning really brings out the best in this photinia, and encourages plenty of bushy and colourful new shoots.

Black-stemmed bamboo
Phyllostachys nigra

Elegant sophistication from a designer evergreen

Time to plant: all year round
Bamboo H: 3–5m (10–16ft), S: 2–3m (6–10ft)

Virtually all bamboos will do well if planted in some shade, as this often means cooler and damper soil, which bamboo roots relish. In recent years this black-stemmed bamboo has become ubiquitous in urban gardens, and no wonder because it is a spectacular example of natural elegance.

The new stems of *Phyllostachys nigra* emerge green but they change over a year or so into the most gorgeous ebony black, which contrasts well with its fresh green foliage. The clump does spread a bit, but is never a nuisance and surplus new stems around the edge can be easily dug up (with some roots attached) and transplanted within your garden or given to friends.

This bamboo also grows very happily in a large container, and it looks especially sleek in a contemporary aluminium planter with a mulch of cobbles on top. Make sure the compost remains damp at all times, though, as potted bamboos need copious amounts of water.

TIP
For a magical night-time effect, position a garden uplighter underneath the plant.

Chusan palm
Trachycarpus fortunei

Create an exotic look with a hardy palm

Time to plant: all year round
Palm H: 21m (70ft), S: 2.4m (8ft)

Tropical is definitely trendy these days, and the sight of this palm instantly evokes much warmer climes. Despite its exotic appearance, it is in fact completely hardy and will happily take a little shade for some of the day. Its pleated fans of evergreen foliage look especially fitting in a small town or courtyard garden, contributing to the external decor right through the year.

Little or no pampering is needed with this palm, just plant it in any reasonably well-drained soil and water it until it becomes established. You can also grow it very easily in a large pot, filled with soil-based compost. This is the best option if you are growing plants in pots long-term, and also makes it easier to keep plants damp in summer.

As it grows the plant will naturally lose its lower leaves to form a bare stem, but you may have to cut them off when they start to go brown in order to keep the plant looking pristine.

TIP
Another hardy palm to try is *Chamerops humilis*, which is similar to *Trachycarpus fortunei*, but more compact.

Flowering quince
Chaenomeles speciosa

Oriental elegance for a shady wall

Time to plant: all year round
Shrub H: 2.4m (8ft), S: 5m (16ft)

The plump buds of this flowering quince unravel their sumptuous petals along its bare stems just as winter slips into spring. Deep red varieties, such as 'Crimson and Gold', are very popular, but you can also get flowers in pink, white and even peachy shades. It's naturally a large, spreading shrub, but it looks so much better when trained onto a wall or fence, even one in quite deep shade.

Growing it on a wall is easy. Attach some horizontal wires or a piece of wooden trellis to the wall first, and then start tying the branches to it during summer with soft string. Each year snip back any excess branches to the main framework after flowering.

Ornamental green quince fruits are usually produced after flowering, and ripen to rich yellow in autumn. These make delicious quince jelly or can be simply left on the plant to provide a bit of extra colour.

TIP
Plant a small-flowered *Clematis viticella* variety nearby to grow into its branches and provide late summer colour, then cut the clematis back to the ground before the quince start flowering.

Alpine clematis
Clematis alpina 'Tage Lundell'

Graceful climber brings colourful perkiness to spring

Time to plant: all year round
Climber (perennial) H: 2–3m (6–10ft),
S: 1.5m (5ft)

Selected for its distinctive dark rose-purple colour, this variety of alpine clematis flowers in spring, when its nodding blooms spangle the delicate stems.

Despite its dainty appearance, this clematis, and all the other *C. alpina* varieties, is pretty tough and can tolerate extremely cold gardens and also a fair degree of shade. Against a wall is an obvious place to plant this clematis, but it also looks pretty cascading over a low retaining wall or spilling over the edge of a tall terracotta pot.

Pruning couldn't be easier – it doesn't need any. If your plant ever needs a bit of a trim to keep it in shape, though, do it after flowering; that way you won't miss out on flowers the following year. If you've had a clematis die from clematis wilt before, you'll be glad to know that this one is completely resistant.

TIP
Don't be too hasty to deadhead spent flowers as they are usually followed by very tactile, feathery seedheads.

Clematis
Clematis x durandii

Cover vertical spaces with indigo blooms

Time to plant: all year round
Climber (perennial) H: 1–2m (3½–6½ft),
S: 1–2m (3½–6½ft)

While most types of clematis prefer to hold their heads in the sun, this pretty hybrid revels in a place where it gets shade for some of the day. From June to September its sumptuously rich indigo flowers appear, revealing a prominent creamy centre that ensures the blooms stand out, however shaded.

This clematis is rather unusual because it's a hybrid between the herbaceous, shrubby, *Clematis integrifolia*, and the climber C. 'Jackmanii'. Its stems are more likely to scramble than climb, and this makes it perfect for growing into a large shrub or over low-growing perennials in a border.

Pruning couldn't be easier. Simply cut all the stems back to nearly ground level in early spring before growth starts; this will result in strong stems from the base, which will still flower in summer. Generous feeding will encourage the best flowering, so mulch around the base every year with well-rotted manure or garden compost. This is especially beneficial in drier soils as it also helps conserve moisture in summer.

TIP
Put up slug barriers when you cut back old growth to prevent slugs nibbling the young shoots as they emerge.

Silk-tassel bush
Garrya elliptica

Hassle-free tassels for a winter wall

Time to plant: all year round
Shrub H: 4m (13ft), S: 4m (13ft)

From winter to early spring, clusters of silvery-green catkins festoon the dark evergreen frame of this large shrub like a cascade of icicles. The best way to appreciate these draping catkins is by growing the plant against a wall, loosely tying in some of the main stems with soft rubber ties. It does especially well against a shady wall or fence, where the pale catkins really shine out for many weeks in winter.

The silk-tassel bush can eventually get quite large, but you can keep it neat and compact by pruning back some of the shoots straight after flowering.

Garrya elliptica does well in almost any well-drained soil, and although it is generally tolerant of wind, cold winds may cause a little scorching on leaves in spring. Choose the variety 'James Roof' when available, as this producers very long catkins.

TIP
Look out for a variety called 'James Roof', which has extra-long tassels.

Variegated ivy
Hedera helix 'Eva'

Versatile evergreen that shines bright from the deepest shade

Time to plant: all year around
Climber H: 1.5m (5ft), S: 1.5m (5ft)

Ivies are synonymous with shade – they simply revel in it. Britain's native ivy, *Hedera helix*, has beautiful, dark green lustrous leaves, but it's the variegated types like this one that really shine out from a shady position in the garden.

The versatility of ivies is amazing and, although they are mostly thought of as climbers, these wonderful evergreens can create brilliant ground cover, even in the dry soil under trees. They are also indispensable for tumbling over the edge of containers, especially in winter pots and baskets, and can even be trained into elaborate topiary with the help of a wire framework. Whichever way they are grown, ivies have a very useful knack of looking good in both traditional and contemporary gardens, and are also very easy to grow.

Very little aftercare is needed once an ivy has established. If you are planting one to grow up a wall there's no need to tie in the shoots because ivy can cling on by means of tiny roots along the stems. At some stage you probably will have to trim off the excess growth when it reaches the top of the wall, but this is a quick and easy job.

TIP
To encourage ivy to stick to a wall, cut back all the stems by about half before planting. The resulting new shoots will then stick to it as they grow, and you'll also get a bushier plant.

Japanese honeysuckle
Lonicera japonica 'Halliana'

An evergreen climber for evening impact

Time to plant: all year round
Climber (perennial) H: 9m (30ft),
S: indefinite

Honeysuckles are natural shade-dwellers, scrambling up through the canopies of trees or into hedges. Unlike our native honeysuckle, *Lonicera japonica* 'Halliana' has the advantage of being evergreen, so it's a good choice if you need to screen off an ugly wall or fence.

Of course this Japanese honeysuckle also lives up to the family's reputation of having a delicious sweet perfume, which wafts around the garden on mild summer evenings. Its pale creamy-yellow flowers are produced all along its twining stems for months in summer, and are a striking colour cutting through the shadows.

You'll need to provide some trellis or wires to help its stems get a hold on a wall or fence, or you could plant one to scramble into a mature tree. If you are growing it on a wall or arch, some pruning is necessary every year just after flowering to prevent it becoming a tangle of stems.

TIP
Mildew is a problem on dry soils, so mulch generously with compost or well-rotted manure every spring to conserve moisture.

Chinese Virginia creeper
Parthenocissus henryana

A climber that crackles with vibrant colour

Time to plant: all year round
Climber (perennial) H: 9m (30ft),
S: indefinite

Silver veins give an extra lift to the
handsome leaves of this Virginia creeper,
especially if it's grown on a shady wall or
fence. As soon as the first chilly nights arrive
in autumn, the leaves go into a slow burn
until the whole plant glows rich crimson.

This self-clinging climber is very easy to
manage once established, but its stems
may need a little coaxing to get them to
adhere to a wall. Cutting all the stems back
by about half before planting is often the
best treatment because its stems need to
start growing against a wall before they will
stick. This pruning seems rather hard, but
it will encourage plenty of new stems from
the base, which will cling to their support
as they grow.

Once a plant reaches the top of a wall
or fence, the surplus stems can be simply
trimmed off in winter or early spring.

TIP
Always plant self-clinging climbers,
such as Virginia creeper, in the ground
rather than a pot as re-potting is almost
impossible once it has taken off.

Firethorn
Pyracantha 'Orange Charmer'

Warm up autumn gardens with fiery berries

Time to plant: all year round
Shrub H: 3m (10ft), S: 3m (10ft)

The zesty orange berries of this evergreen shrub almost seem to glow in a shady autumn area. Although it can be grown as an ordinary shrub in a large border, it's magnificent if trained on a wall, even one facing north, when you will get the full visual benefit of its berry-laden branches.

Keeping a pyracantha flat against a wall isn't difficult, all you need to do is attach a few horizontal wires or a piece of trellis to the wall and tie in the stems during summer. As the plant gets older or fills its allocated space, you'll have excess shoots to deal with and these can be simply snipped off after flowering. The clusters of white flowers, incidentally, are rather like pretty hawthorn blossom and wreathe the stems in early summer.

TIP
Wear gloves when pruning as the evergreen branches have plenty of thorns.

Schizophragma
Schizophragma integrifolium

Get a high-rise performance in late summer

Time to plant: all year round
Climber (perennial) H: 12m (40ft),
S: indefinite

This is a wonderful alternative to the climbing hydrangea for a shady wall. *Schizophragma integrifolium* looks quite similar, but its lacecap flowerheads are larger and more dramatic. What's more, the papery-white bracts around the outside of each flowerhead last much longer before fading – often as long as two or three months.

A large wall is the ideal place to plant this attractive climber; there it has room to show its true magnificence. *Schizophragma* can be pruned to keep it a little more compact if necessary, and this is best done in spring when you should shorten shoots and cut back an occasional older stem.

Soil that stays slightly damp in summer suits this plant best, so add plenty of compost when planting and, in drier soils, use a heavy mulch of compost every year.

An alternative and very natural use for this climber is to plant it beside a mature tree, and coax its stems to cling to its host with a bit of temporary support. It can take a few years to really get going, but once it starts flowering the effect is spectacular.

TIP
Look out for a very snazzy pink-flowered schizophragma called *S. hydrangeoides* 'Roseum' – it will become a real talking point on a shady wall.

Black-eyed Susan
Thunbergia alata 'Superstar'

Cover blank walls with a dark-eyed summer beauty

Time to plant: after the last frosts in early summer
Climber (perennial) H: 2.4m (8ft), S: indefinite

Once a plant you would only expect to see in a conservatory, this beautiful climber is much more versatile than that and can be used to great effect outdoors during summer. It is striking when trained up an obelisk, positioned either in a border or pots, and it will even grow well in a large hanging basket, from which its wickedly dark-centred orange flowers can cascade. Best of all, it will even bring its sunny charms to a spot in partial shade.

Thunbergia alata 'Superstar' is a new, large-flowered selection of black-eyed Susan. Although it's a perennial if it is overwintered indoors, it's often just as easy to raise plants afresh from seed each year. Sow seed indoors during spring and plant out in the garden in early summer, after the risk of frost has passed.

TIP
Sow the seeds thinly and transplant to individual pots as soon as they are large enough to handle.

Star jasmine
Trachelospermum jasminoides

Fill your garden with wall-to-wall fragrance

Time to plant: all year round
Climber (perennial) H: 9m (30ft),
S: indefinite

Shaped like tiny white propellers, the
flowers of this evergreen climber seem to
fan their exotic fragrance far into the late
summer garden. It's perfectly suited to
grow on an east- or west-facing wall that
is shaded for some of the day, however too
much shade may cause it to have plenty
of leaves and few flowers.

A few wires attached to the wall or fence
will provide plenty of support – in fact
the stems of star jasmine can be almost
self-supporting against a vertical surface.
This climber is actually quite a vigorous
grower when planted in any well-drained
soil and, in addition to the obvious
attraction of its flowers, is well worth
growing because it makes a very dense,
leafy covering all through the year.

No regular pruning is required, but you
may need to trim it to size at some stage.
This is best done in early spring.

TIP
Young plants establish quickly, but it
may be a couple of years before they put
on a good show of flowers.

Bugle
Ajuga reptans 'Black Scallop'

For a low-maintenance bed, try this dark evergreen carpet

Time to plant: all year round
Perennial H: 15cm (6in), S: 90cm (3ft)

This dark new variety of ajuga is sure to turn heads with its inky, evergreen foliage that forms a gorgeous, glossy carpet right through the year. Like all other ajugas, 'Black Scallop' thrives in shade, especially if the soil stays slightly damp during summer. So if you have dry shade, mix in plenty of organic matter when planting.

To make the most of its dark leaves, plant this ajuga alongside contrasting foliage plants, such as the electric-blue *Corydalis flexuosa* and golden grasses such as *Milium effusum* 'Aureum', which also do well in the shade. Small spikes of blue flowers rise above the leaves in late spring and early summer.

In spring you can make more ajuga plants for free simply by digging up and detaching the sections of its spreading stems that have already rooted in the soil.

TIP
A mulch of pale pebble chippings around the plant will help the leaves stand out.

Elephant's ears
Bergenia x *schmidtii*

Make space for a rounded character at the front of a border

Time to plant: all year round
Perennial H: 30cm (12in), S: 60cm (2ft)

Bergenia was a favourite of the great plantswoman Gertrude Jekyll, who created many spectacular gardens early in the last century. This bergenia has the knack of looking great right through the year; its round, leathery, evergreen leaves form delightful patches of green that are perfect for softening the edges of paths or patios. What's more, the so-called elephant's ears can grow in quite heavy shade and are very dependable in cold, windy gardens.

Stout stems carrying sprays of clear pink flowers rise just above the leaves in spring, often as early as February, and like many other bergenias the leaves are usually suffused with maroon shades during winter.

Bergenia thrives in any well-drained soil and tolerates dry shade remarkably well; it also demands no regular care, apart from trimming off the old flowerheads.

TIP
Old clumps will flower better if they are dug up in early spring, split up into smaller sections and then replanted into compost-enriched soil.

Brunnera
Brunnera macrophylla 'Jack Frost'

Let frosty patterns provide some winter sparkle

Time to plant: all year round
Perennial H: 45cm (18in), S: 60cm (2ft)

Reliably tough even in poor soil, this perennial shows its daintier side when sprays of blue forget-me-not flowers shimmer over its large, bristly leaves in spring. Brunnera is an excellent plant for using in the soft, dappled shade at the edge of tree canopies, and it looks wonderful skirting around the base of a white-stemmed birch (*Betula*).

There are a couple of variegated types available, but look out for this new variety, 'Jack Frost', which has silver patterns on the leaves. This sensational foliage will shine out even from deep shade and look great for most of the year. A quick tidy up in late autumn, once the leaves do start to die back, is all the care this plant requires.

If you ever need a few new plants, simply dig up the parent plant in spring, just as new growth starts, and split it into a few sections. Make sure each piece has some shoots and roots, and then replant in the garden.

TIP
Plant several brunneras together in a large group for efficient, weed-suppressing ground cover.

Lily-of-the-valley
Convallaria majalis

Tiny bells that are big on scent

Time to plant: autumn
Perennial H: 23cm (9in), S: 30cm (12in)

The tiny, pristine white, waxy bells of this well-known flower are custodians to one of the loveliest fragrances found in the garden. Pick a few sprigs when they are in flower in early summer and place them in a tiny jar so that you can fully appreciate all its gentle nuances. The plant itself has a much more robust nature and forms dense ground cover, even in deep shade.

The leaves of lily-of-the-valley aren't evergreen, but few weeds can get a foothold once its underground stems have matted together beneath the surface. This plant does best in heavy, but not wet, soils and is excellent skirting around the base of tall shrubs. Pieces of roots (really underground stems) are available in the autumn and should be planted horizontally just below the surface in well-prepared, compost-enriched soil.

TIP
Pot up a few pieces of its roots in winter and place in a cold greenhouse, or unheated porch, for an earlier display of deliciously perfumed flowers.

Creeping dogwood
Cornus canadensis

A dainty dogwood that turns on the charm

Time to plant: all year round
Perennial H: 15cm (6in), S: indefinite

Only when the tell-tale, pretty white flowers appear in early summer does this low, creeping perennial reveal itself as a member of the magnificent, flowering, dogwood family. The petals of creeping dogwood are, in fact, bracts that last much longer than petals, and these surround a button-shaped cluster of actual flowers in the centre.

Once these flowers are over, small clusters of red fruit spangle the lush green leaves, which have wonderful autumn tints. Thanks to a network of underground stems, its semi-evergreen leaves soon make very dense ground cover, especially in the cool, leafy soil under trees.

Once established, creeping dogwood needs virtually no attention, but don't let young plants dry out if you are planting them during the summer months.

TIP
This cornus does best in peaty, acid soil, so add some ericaceous compost to the soil when planting.

Bishop's mitre
Epimedium perralderianum

Hold back weeds with a dainty-flowered evergreen

Time to plant: all year round
Perennial H: 30cm (12in), S: 60cm (2ft)

Weeds get little chance to squeeze through the deep evergreen carpet of this tough perennial. Bishop's mitre is particularly at home in a shady position, and it is invaluable as a permanent under-storey to trees and in situations where you want to keep maintenance levels low.

Despite its robust nature, *Epimedium perralderianum* also has a more delicate side, which is revealed in spring when sprays of exquisitely detailed yellow flowers rise just above the leaves. Unlike some of the non-evergreen epimediums, which can have their old foliage clipped away each winter, this one can be left unclipped as it looks handsome all through winter.

Bishop's mitre thrives in almost any soil but it does best in places that don't get too dry in summer. A mulch of compost every spring is beneficial to young plants until they establish.

TIP
When buying plants, choose pots containing plenty of shoots and then divide the plant into smaller sections. These pieces can then be planted as a group, which will cover the ground faster.

Sweet woodruff
Galium odoratum

A scented ground cover with a whorl of a difference

Time to plant: all year round
Perennial H: 45cm (18in), S: indefinite

Whorls of fresh apple-green foliage act as the perfect under-storey to the frothy heads of scented white flowers that open in early summer on this pretty perennial. Sweet woodruff positively thrives in shade and is especially suitable for a semi-wild woodland situation among shrubs, where it forms a sheet of white when flowering.

Damp soil encourages plenty of lush leaves and flowers, although sweet woodruff will grow in drier soils too, especially when planted in cool, deep shade. You will often find small plants for sale in the herb section at the garden centre as *Galium odoratum* does have some medicinal and herbal qualities. These young plants establish quickly if planted in compost-enriched soil, but they will also grow well in a pot if they are placed out of direct sun – the advantage of this is that they won't take over if you have a small garden.

TIP
Pick and dry some of the flowering stems to bring a sweet smell of fresh hay to potpourri.

Coral flower
Heuchera 'Color Dream'

Plant sumptuous purple leaves for summer

Time to plant: all year round
Perennial H: 45cm (18in), S: 45cm (18in)

Scalloped leaves patterned with purple and overlaid with a silvery sheen ensure this new heuchera variety has quickly become a favourite for pots and borders. Like all heucheras, it luxuriates in a little cool shade and its slender spires of white bells bring extra light to summer.

During summer the leaves develop a distinctive red edge, which, like a vivid lipstick, gives the whole plant a perky lift. These leaves are also evergreen and can make quite good ground cover when plants are grouped together.

Any well-drained soil suits this easily grown perennial, but don't allow the plant to become too dry during summer. A mulch of compost will help to conserve moisture during the drier months. Heucheras are easy to grow in pots, and they are invaluable for adding a sumptuous splash of purple foliage to winter containers.

TIP
Take precautions against vine weevil grubs, which can nibble their way through the entire root system, especially in pots.

Hosta
Hosta 'Orange Marmalade'

Create a bold impact with lush foliage

Time to plant: all year round
Perennial H: 60cm (2ft), S: 90cm (3ft)

This big, bold and undeniably beautiful hybrid is the ultimate foliage plant for a shady border. Hundreds of different varieties are available, some with simple green or golden leaves, others with striking variegations, and then there are the wonderful chalky blue-leaved varieties. All hostas provide interest for ages, right from early spring when their pointed, purple buds break through the soil until late autumn when ochre shades seep into the leaves.

Hostas are mostly grown for their foliage, but they all carry small, trumpet-shaped flowers on strong stems above the leaves in summer, and these can be white or purplish and are sometimes scented. Slugs love hostas, but they tend to dislike the tough-leaved blue varieties while pot-grown specimens often escape their attention.

TIP
Established hostas are quite heavy to dig up and divide. Instead, slice off a section with a stout knife or spade just when the buds emerge. This can be used without disturbing the main plant.

Deadnettle
Lamium maculatum 'Album'

Add sparkle to deepest shade

Time to plant: all year round
Perennial H: 15cm (6in), S: 60cm (2ft)

The common name of deadnettle may not instil much confidence, but this easily grown perennial is one of the very best plants for growing in deep shade.
In addition to the silvery splotch on the leaf that is common to many varieties, 'Album' has the added bonus of glistening white flowers in early summer that sparkle from the gloom.

Like most varieties, its nearly indestructible nature, combined with a spreading habit, make it invaluable as ground cover in poor soils and shady areas. The leafy stems aren't evergreen, but 'Album' makes such a dense mat for most of the year that few weeds can stake their claim.

If new plants are ever required, simply dig up a clump in spring and split it into small sections, ensuring each piece has some roots and a few shoots.

TIP
Cut back leggy stems after flowering to encourage a fresh flush of foliage from the base.

Pachysandra
Pachysandra terminalis

A ground controller to tackle tough jobs

Time to plant: all year round
Perennial H: 20cm (8in), S: indefinite

Toughness seems to be instilled in this evergreen perennial, as it manages to perform even in the most difficult of dry, shady places. In fact, pachysandra is just the sort of plant to choose if you have dense, overhanging trees and you think nothing else will grow underneath. It's also a very good carpeting plant and will provide excellent weed-suppressing ground cover once established.

The tops of its low, creeping stems become studded with clusters of tiny white flowers in early summer – a lovely bonus above shiny green foliage and easy to spot, even in deep shade. There is also a variegated variety available that has attractive, white-margined leaves which really brighten up a shady spot, but it's not as vigorous as the green-leaved type.

TIP
Although pachysandra is tolerant of very poor soil, give each plant a good start by adding plenty of compost to the soil when planting.

Lungwort
Pulmonaria longifolia

Add a little glitz to a shady spot

Time to plant: all year round
Perennial H: 30cm (12in), S: 45cm (18in)

Silver-speckled leaves ensure this handsome perennial brings a little bling to a shady garden. Its long leaves, slightly bristly to the touch, form very lush rosettes that are accompanied by sprays of beautiful blue flowers in early spring. These last for several weeks and are lovely as an under-storey to dwarf golden daffodils, such as 'February Gold'.

Like all pulmonarias, *Pulmonaria longifolia* will grow much better when it can sink its toes into cool, damp soil. If the ground is too dry you may get mildew on the leaves, so in drier soils mulch generously with compost every year to help conserve moisture. Very little other care is required apart from tidying back old flower stems and leaves in winter.

Most pulmonarias self-seed generously about the garden, but to get new plants from named forms it is best to divide plants in autumn. If planted as a group, pulmonarias will form excellent ground cover.

TIP

The red-flowered *Pulmonaria rubra* is a very useful, evergreen pulmonaria which also makes excellent ground cover under trees.

London pride
Saxifraga x *urbium* 'Variegata'

Create colourful carpets with a cottage-garden favourite

Time to plant: all year round
Perennial H: 30cm (12in), S: indefinite

A long-standing favourite of the cottage garden, this evergreen perennial has an endearing habit of being able to grow almost anywhere in the garden, especially in deep shade. The gold-speckled leaves look particularly attractive in shade, and form dense rosettes over which hover airy sprays of dainty blush flowers in summer.

Over time, and especially if planted as a group, the slightly fleshy leaf rosettes of London pride knit tightly together to make excellent ground cover. It's lovely under the arms of large shrubs or as an edging to a bed, where it can spill out to soften the line of a path. You may have to act as referee if it's planted among choice perennials, but surplus bits around the edge of the clump are easy to dig up, if necessary.

TIP
Rosettes with some roots attached can be detached almost at any time of year and planted elsewhere, or be given to friends.

Comfrey
Symphytum 'Hidcote Blue'

Welcome wildlife with woodland plants

Time to plant: all year round
Perennial H: 45cm (18in), S: 45cm (18in)

Early, foraging bees love to delve into the nodding blue bells of this pretty comfrey during spring, so it's very suitable for planting in a wildlife-friendly garden, especially in a woodland setting. There are several different types of comfrey, some with white or red flowers and others with variegated foliage that pack a punch in a dull border.

Established plants make lush, leafy clumps that need a bit of elbow room in a border, but this comfrey is perhaps best used for ground cover under trees, or for naturalising in a semi-wild garden.

Damp soil is essential, but otherwise this hearty perennial makes few demands and is very easy to grow. If you ever need a few extra plants, dig up and divide an established specimen during spring, just as growth starts.

TIP
Cut back the whole plant to the ground in summer to encourage a new flush of foliage.

Foam flower
Tiarella 'Iron Butterfly'

Fill beds with frothy flowers

Time to plant: all year round
Perennial H: 30cm (12in), S: 30cm (12in)

New varieties of the foam flower, including 'Iron Butterfly' with its chocolate-patterned leaves, have made this gentle little woodland plant a choice addition to a shady border. Several spikes of white flowers rise above the foliage in spring, making a frothy contribution for many weeks.

If planted as a group, tiarellas make excellent ground cover, which is especially useful in a tricky, shady area under trees. Once established the only attention this perennial needs is when dead leaves are trimmed off in winter. Plants can be lifted and divided if necessary in spring, replanting strong pieces back into compost-enriched soil.

TIP
This plant looks best en masse, so plant several together in a group for a really bold effect.

Foam Flower

Tiarella 'Tiger Stripe'

Make a bold statement in dull borders

Time to plant: all year round
Perennial H: 25cm (10in), S: 30cm (12in)

Many new varieties of the common foam flower have appeared in recent years, and this stands out as one of the best because of its handsome foliage, boldly marked with an inky pattern in the centre. The leaves remain evergreen during winter, often turning darker in the colder months. Like the entire family, it too revels in a bit of shade and does well under trees.

If several plants are arranged in a group, *Tiarella* 'Tiger Stripe' can make an attractive ground cover when it is sprinkled with pinkish-white foamy flowers in spring. This is an easy-natured perennial that only needs a little tidy up of dead leaves or old flower stems once it has established itself.

Old clumps can be dug up and divided in spring if new plants are required. Replant strong pieces straight away in compost-enriched soil, and water well until established.

TIP

Tiarellas like damp, organic-rich soil so mulch generously with garden compost if planting them in a dry spot.

x Heucherella
x *Heucherella* 'Sunspot'

Bring sunshine to shade

Time to plant: all year round
Perennial H: 45cm (18in), S: 45cm (18in)

Golden-leaved plants often do best in some shade, and this new variety of x *Heucherella* is no exception.
Its gold-suffused evergreen leaves are less liable to scorch when placed out of direct sun, and its roots also prefer to grow in cool, leafy soil.

A hybrid between a heuchera and tiarella, x *Heucherella* 'Sunspot' shares its parents' hardy nature and is a reliable, trouble-free perennial that gets better every year.
The flowers appear on slender stems and are fairly subtle, but they are a welcome bonus during summer.

TIP
Use its bright foliage in winter pots among dark, velvety-blue pansies and lush, evergreen ferns.

Index

Picture credits

BBC Books and *Gardeners' World Magazine* would like to thank the following for providing photographs. While every effort has been made to trace and acknowledge all photographers, we should like to apologize should there be any errors or omissions.

Peter Anderson p81; BBC Books p57, p59; Ray Cox p77; Eric Crichton p157, p183, p189; Eric Crichton/BBC Books p173; Sarah Cuttle p23, p63, p141, p165; Paul Debois p29, p35, p39, p205; Peter Durkes p185; *Gardeners' World Magazine* p13, p33, p119, p187; Caroline Hughes p99, p131; Anne Hyde p71, p73; Anne Hyde/Haydon Nursery p85; Jason Ingram p19, p21, p31, p43, p45, p53, p65, p83, p91, p109, p135, p145, p147, p195, p207; Lynn Keddie p179; David Murray p69, p193; Adrian Myers p121;

Stephen Robson p153; Sabina Ruber p127; Tim Sandall p15, p17, p27, p49, p51, p79, p87, p89, p105, p113, p117, p123, p129, p133, p139, p149, p151, p161, p169, p175, p209; Jane Sebire p107, William Shaw p47, p95, p143; John Trenholm P25, p55, p61, p97, p101, p211; Jo Whitworth p11, p37, p41, p75, p93, p103, p111, p115, p125, p137, p155, p159, p163, p167, p171, p177, p181, p191, p197, p199, p201, p203; Mark Winwood p67